YUM
YUM
I0820573
WOW
WOW
YUM
YUM
YUM
YUM
YAY
YAY

GUINEA PIG
CAVIA TSCHUDII
PERUVIAN ANCHOVETA
ENGRAULIS RINGENS
HUMMINGBIRD
LODDIGESIA MIRABILIS
SEA LION
ARCTOCEPHALUS AUSTRALIS
SEAGULL
LARUS BELCHERI
PERUVIAN DESERT FOX
LYCALOPEX SECHURAE
HUMBOLDT PENGUIN
SPHENISCUS HUMBOLDTI
SPECTACLED BEAR
TREMARCTOS ORNATUS
LLAMA
LAMA GLAMA

PÍA LEÓN AND MALENA MARTÍNEZ

feast

RECIPES AND SUPERFOODS FROM PERU

PICHONCITO

PÍA

FOR CRISTOBAL, WHOM I
MOST ENJOY COOKING FOR
AND WHOSE OPINION ON THE
RESULTS IS THE ONE I VALUE
MOST IN THE WORLD.

MALENA

FOR INÉS, WHO IS WILLING TO
TRY QUINOAS OF DIFFERENT
COLORS, SACHA TOMATE JAM,
COCONA JUICE, AND SAYS YUMMY!
EVERY SINGLE TIME.

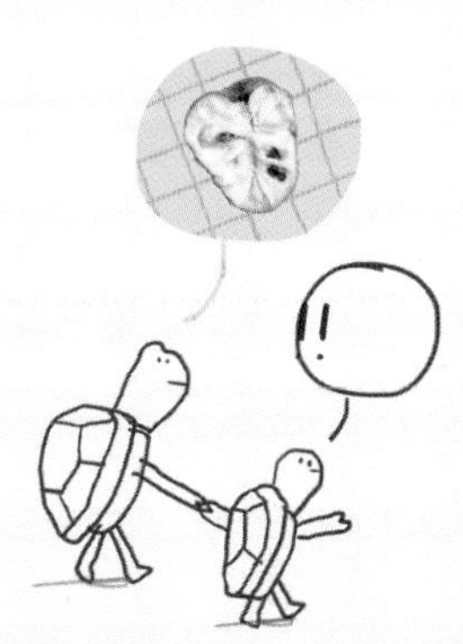

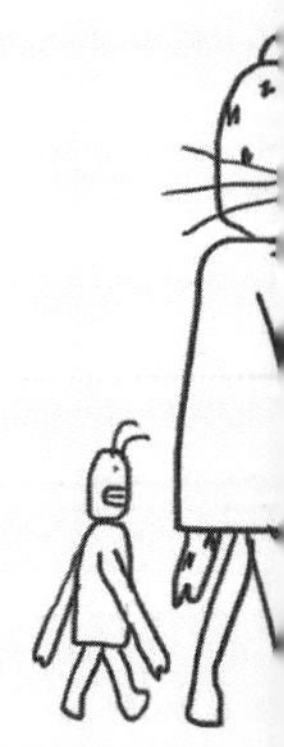

CASA
TÚPAC

FEAST

Authors:
© Pía León
© Malena Martínez

Editors: Adriana Roca and Karina Villalba
Art Direction: Raquel Tudela
Illustration, Design and Layout: Melissa Siles
Photography: Jimena Agois
Style Editor: Jorge Cornejo
Writing Assistant: Michela Melzi
Photographic Retouch: John Smith Cerquín
Translated: María Fe Carranza
Copy Editor: Samantha Lewis

Edited by Ediciones Pichoncito S. A. C.
Jr. Santa Rosa 359, Barranco, Lima, Peru
www.pichoncito.pe
R. U. C. 20603234643

First edition: May 2025
Print run: 2,000 copies
Printed at Corporate Graphics Commercial
1750 Northway Drive
North Mankato, MN 56003
United States
May 2025
ISBN: 978-612-4450-57-0
Legal deposit at the National Library of Peru n.° 2024-12354.

WELCOME TO THE feast

id you know that *cushuros*, an edible algae that resembles perfect pearls, grow on the shores of lakes and rivers in the central Andes? Did you know that in the mountains of Peru more than 4000 varieties of potatoes grow in different shapes, sizes, colors, and consistencies? Or did you know that in the Peruvian Amazon the *macambo* grows, a fruit closely related to cacao, that is used to prepare delicious drinks?

In Peru, all climates and regions meet. We have the sea, desert, Andean mountains, and tropical rainforest. A great variety of flora and fauna grow in its prodigious lands and warm waters, plants and animals.

Peru's biodiversity is famous worldwide because of talented researchers and chefs. Researchers rediscovered and studied ancient ingredients. Chefs used these ingredients with both traditional and modern cooking techniques, their own experiences, and other influences to create what is now recognized as some of the tastiest and most innovative food in the world.

This book celebrates the talents and flavors of Peru. It celebrates the diversity of its Coast, its Andes, and its Jungle. It celebrates cooking with family, cooking with friends, cooking with love, and curiosity. It celebrates sharing values and learning. It celebrates gathering around the table to savor, discover, and have fun.

Join the party! Explore the Coast, the Mountains, and the Jungle through their culinary richness, and discover all the flavors waiting for you in each recipe. A true feast!

MALENA

Hi, I'm Malena! I am a scientist and I love to research! My favorite color is green: the green of forest leaves and many other wonders that grow in nature. Maybe that´s why I am fascinated by botany, agriculture, and discovering what we can create in our kitchens with the ingredients from our vast and rich country. In Peru, there are thousands of ecosystems that create many varieties of delicious potatoes, corn, avocados, and many more products. For example, we have quinoa, but not only the white, red, and black kinds. We have hundreds of different types that are sometimes named after the places they grow.

In this book, we'll introduce you to 21 superfoods of ancient origin that are extremely rich in nutrients and are native to the different regions of Peru. We invite you to explore Peruvian markets and wander through their aisles full of aromas and vibrant colors. Taste a great variety of products that you never knew existed and share beautiful and age-old Peruvian traditions that grow every day around the world.

Stay curious. The magic of cooking resides in discovering new ingredients, new combinations, new smells, new experiences. Use these recipes as a guide, but always feel free to add your personal touch. Food is an art, like music or dancing. Be free. Don't ever stop dancing, singing, or cooking.

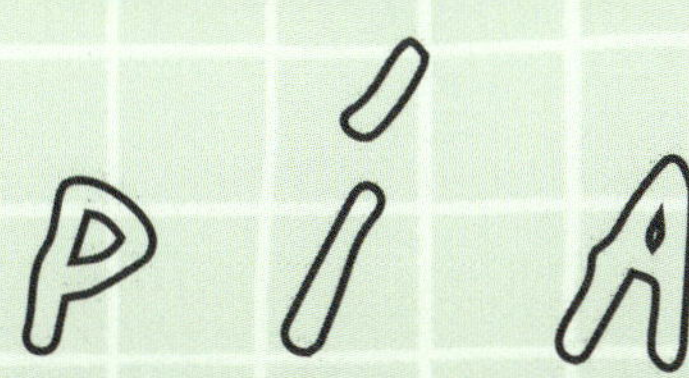

Hi! My name is Pía. I have loved cooking ever since I was a little girl. My mom would spend every weekend making something delicious, and I was always by her side, watching. I love being in the kitchen, where everything is in constant motion and you can find delicious smells and flavors, and create special memories and endearing moments.

What´s my favorite recipe? Phew! I have many, but I think the one I like the most is *locro*, a squash stew. It is simple and tasty, and it's my son Cristóbal's favorite. My favorite food? Andean corn! Add a little salt and ta-da, you have a delicious dish! What a coincidence, they are both yellow, my favorite color!

I invite you to discover fun recipes in this book, my first for children! The recipes were inspired by every single one of the magical regions in Peru and created with Malena´s well-researched superfoods. Go for it! Give in, be risky and above all, have fun! I recommend cooking with music, friends, family, and sharing what you cook with the people you care for most. That´s the best part!

WE'LL PREPARE FUN AND DELICIOUS PURPLE RECIPES WITH THEM!

!!

BEFORE WE BEGIN...

Cooking is like a game; it has important rules that you probably already know:

SAFETY MEASURES

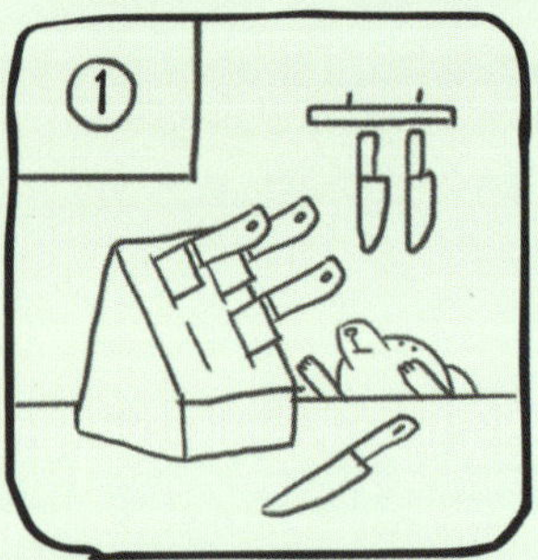

Be careful when using knives and sharp objects.

Keep the kitchen floor dry and obstacle-free.

Use gloves or oven mitts to handle hot containers from the oven.

Avoid contact between raw and cooked foods to avoid cross-contamination.

Keep your distance from the stove and from any containers with hot water.

HELP! In the recipes you'll find this drawing ⚠ whenever a step or procedure requires the help or supervision of an adult. Pay attention!

SETUP

Prepare the foods you'll need for the recipe ahead of time: weigh and process them (wash, peel, grate, chop, or cut) as directed. If any step is too hard, ask for help.

ABBREVIATIONS AND EQUIVALENCIES

tbsp.	tablespoon	oz	ounces
tsp.	teaspoon	cup	cup
g	gram	lb	pounds

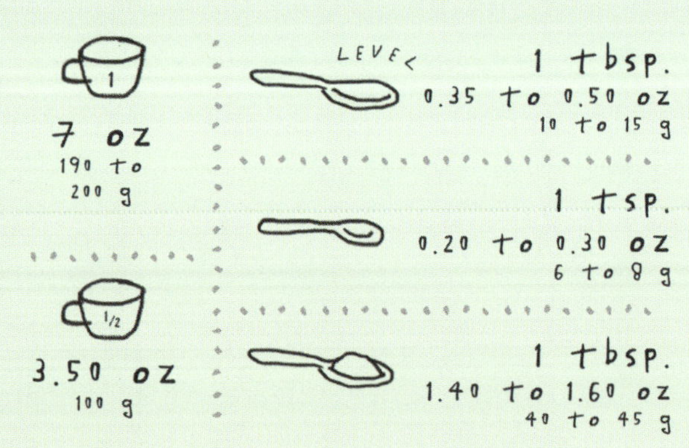

1. Scale. 2. Hand mixer. 3. Electric mixer. 4. Bowl. 5. Regular and thin strainer. 6. Dessert glasses. 7. Spoon, wooden spoon, and ladle. 8. Knife. 9. Silicone spatula. 10. Squeezer. 11. Baking sheet or tray. 12. Gloves. 13. Blender. 14. Microwave oven. 15. Nonstick molds. 16. Pot (large, medium, and small). 17. Paper (paper towel, aluminum foil, and parchment paper). 18. Stewpot. 19. Potato Press. 20. Grater. 21. Glass container. 22. Clock (stopwatch or timer). 23. Rolling pin. 24. Nonstick frying pan (medium and large). 25. Chopping boards (for fruits and vegetables as well as for meats and fish). 26. Measuring cup.

GLOSSARY

Prep time. Indicates the preparation times and any extra time a procedure could require.

Servings. Indicates how many people you can share your recipe with.

★★ **Difficulty level.** Indicates how easy or complicated each recipe is. Fewer stars means the recipe is easier.

1

2
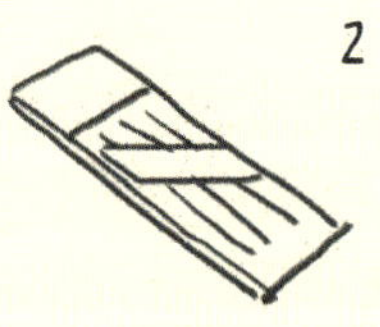

3

4
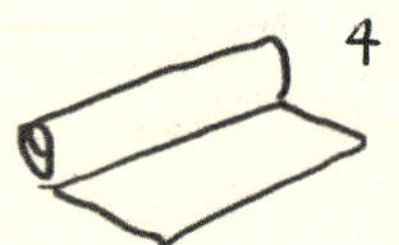

Powdered sugar. A type of sugar generally used in pastries.

Water bath. This technique consists of cooking food in a dish placed in a pan of boiling water to cook it gently and evenly. *fig. 1*

Mandoline slicer. Kitchen utensil that allows foods to be cut with precision into even sheets, slices, or strands. *fig. 2*

Chantilly consistency. Beat cold heavy cream and sugar for a few minutes until it becomes fluffy and spongy. *fig. 3*

Nappe consistency. A technique for sauces to thicken the mixture by stirring constantly over heat. Test by running a finger across the back of the spoon; if it leaves a line, it's ready.

Buttercream consistency. Term that refers to softened and uniform butter, in between solid and liquid forms.

Reduction. A technique that consists of letting a preparation boil —sauce, cream, syrup, or broth— until it decreases in volume and the flavor intensifies.

Rest. Let the preparation rest.

Set aside. Term that indicates when a food or mixture must be placed aside, waiting for the next steps in the recipe.

Silpat. A nonstick silicone baking sheet. *fig. 4*

INGREDIENT ALTERNATIVES

(*) WHEREVER YOU ARE.

CHIRIMOYA OR CUSTARD APPLE		SOURSOP OR GUANABANA, MANGO OR BANANA.	
AROMATIC HERBS		USE THE ONES YOU PREFER. YOU CAN REPLACE OREGANO WITH ROSEMARY, THYME, OR PARSLEY.	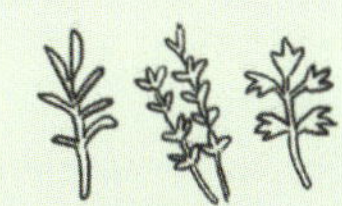
INSTANT OATMEAL		OAT FLOUR, CORN STARCH, OR ANY OTHER CEREAL FLOUR.	
FISH		ALWAYS CHOOSE THE FRESHEST IN YOUR REGION. RESPECT THE CLOSED SEASONS, WHICH ARE PERIODS OF TIME IN WHICH CERTAIN SPECIES MUST NOT BE CAUGHT TO ENSURE THEIR PRESERVATION.	
FRESH CHEESE	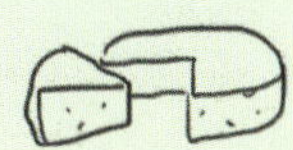	ANY CHEESE WORKS (RICOTTA CHEESE, MOZZARELLA CHEESE, QUESO FRESCO CHEESE).	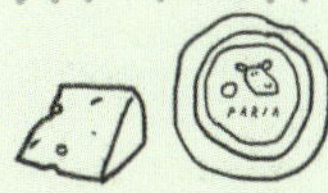
PRICKLY PEAR		DRAGON FRUIT OR KIWI.	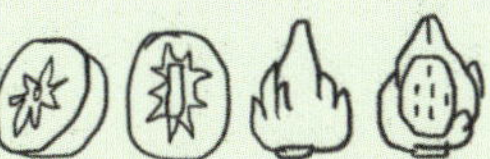
LOCHE SQUASH	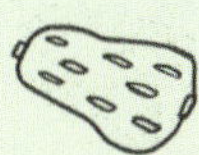	ANY OTHER SQUASH VARIETY.	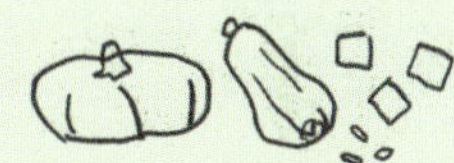

TIPS

To peel a prickly pear: Rub the prickly pears with a paper towel to remove the thorns. Then peel them carefully.

Peruvian yellow chili pepper or yellow ají paste: In a pot filled with water, place three yellow chili peppers, halved and seeded, and wait for the water to boil. Then drain the peppers, discard the water, and repeat. This helps reduce the spiciness. Blend the peppers with a little bit of water until a paste is formed.

Boiling sweet potatoes: You can do this two ways. In a pot with boiling water for 10 minutes at medium heat; or in the microwave, in a bag with little holes, for 10 minutes at medium power.

When the recipe does not specify quantities, it means that you can use the ingredients to taste.

Keep in mind that for a dessert to be a success, the ingredients must have the exact quantities.

Remember that preparation and cooking times are suggested. These may vary depending on the power of each oven and stove.

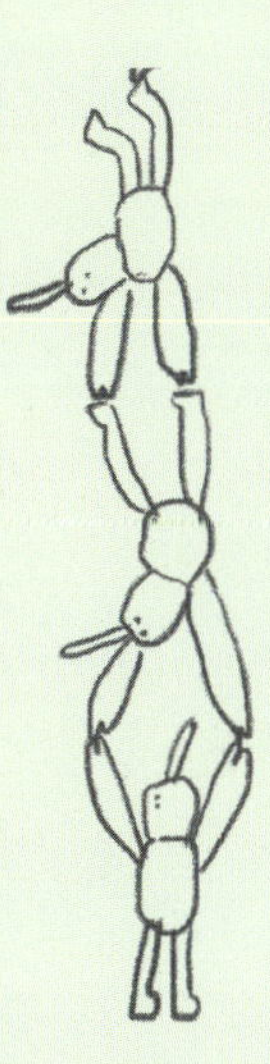

INDEX

COAST 14

LIMA BEAN CEVICHE 20
CAUSA WITH PERUVIAN YELLOW CHILI PEPPER 22
TORTILLAS AND FISH 24
SQUASH AND CHEESE STEW 26
RED AND GREEN PRICKLY PEAR SNOW GRANITE 28
SWEET POTATO MUNCHKINS 30
LUCUMA GUMMIES 32

MOUNTAINS 34

ANDEAN CORN DIP 40
NATIVE POTATO PIZZA 42
OCA DOUGHNUTS 44
GIANT ANDEAN CEREALS COOKIE 46
PURPLE MASHUA ICE CREAM 48
MUÑA LEMONADE 50
CHILLED CHIRIMOYA CREAM 52
QUINOA MINICAKES 54

JUNGLE 56

YUCA CHIPS WITH AVOCADO CREAM AND SACHA CULANTRO 62
SACHA TOMATE RED SAUCE FOR PASTA 64
CACAO CREAM 66
AMAZONIAN CHESTNUT ICE CREAM 68

COAST

From the carob tree forests in northern Peru, all the way down to Ilo, the Coast is home to a desert that occupies 10% of the national territory. The coastline has over 1081 species of fish, 1071 types of mollusks, 625 types of algae, and 53 valleys that produce some of the most delicious and sought-after fruits and vegetables in the world. We invite you to travel the Coast with us and discover its superfoods, along with the fun and delicious recipes you can make with them.

!!
PRICKLY PEAR
THE FEMALE MUY MUY OR PACIFIC SAND CRAB IS ALMOST TWICE THE SIZE OF ITS MALE COUNTERPART.
ROSITA
LÚCUMAS
YUMMY!
THE NATIONAL PARACAS RESERVE IS A PROTECTED AREA LOCATED IN THE PROVINCE OF PISCO.
HURRY UP MOMMY!
SWEET POTATO
EGGS
YEAST

Superfoods from

1. TUMBO OR BANANA PASSION FRUIT

This climbing liana, which can reach up to 33 ft (10 m) in length, grows in the Andes between 5,900 ft (1800 m) and 11154 ft (3400 m) above sea level. It produces flowers and fruits all year long. The passiflora, like the tumbo, passion fruit, or sweet granadilla, are a family of plants with large and beautiful flowers. They received their name from Jesuit missionaries, who were reminded of the passion of Christ. Its fruits are delicious and very nutritious (they are rich in vitamin A, which helps with our vision and concentration), and they can be eaten directly or in juices and desserts.

THE LIMA BEANS MAIN ROOT REACHES UP TO 5 FT (1.5 M) IN DEPTH, BUT HAS MANY SECONDARY ROOTS.

2. LIMA BEANS OR BUTTER BEANS

This high-protein legume has a subtle flavor without the bitterness of others like it, and has a soft, creamy texture when it is cooked. The lima bean plant requires moderate temperatures, relatively high humidity, and lots of light to grow, finding all these attributes in the valley of Ica. Its main root reaches up to 5 ft (1.5 m) in depth, but it has many secondary roots. The lima bean was very important in the prehispanic diet, especially in the Paracas, Nazca, and Moche cultures; it was used by priests to establish a dialogue with the gods and through these, they were able to predict the outcome of the harvest. They are used today, for example, to prepare a succulent *tacu tacu* or a delicious lima bean ceviche!

3. CHARELA

This smooth, scaled fish can dive up to 90 ft (30 m) deep in the ocean and it lives in coastal waters. It is a carnivore (it has a pair of very sharp canine teeth!) and it feeds on mollusks, crustaceans, and small fish. The charela has very high quantities of B vitamins and omega 3.

HERE ARE A FEW TIPS TO MAKE SURE IT'S FRESH:

- The eyes should be shiny.
- The meat must be firm (not soft).
- The gills (through which fish breathe) must have a fresh smell and be red.
- Be sure to buy the whole fish and have it filleted in front of you.

FLAGSHIP OF PERUVIAN CUISINE

4. PERUVIAN YELLOW CHILI PEPPER OR YELLOW AJÍ

What do *ají de gallina, huancaína sauce, arroz con pollo, lomo saltado,* and *cau cau* have in common? They all use the Peruvian yellow chili pepper! A flagship ingredient of Peruvian cuisine, whose spiciness comes from the capsaicinoids that are found in the plant. You can also find a substance called capsaicin, which can be used to treat body aches.

The Peruvian yellow chili pepper has been used in Peru since pre-Inca times. Ancient Peruvians, besides eating it, incorporated it in many rituals, and during the Inca Empire, cultivating it became one of the most important tasks.

COAST

ANTI-INFLAMMATORY

5. SWEET POTATO

The sweet potato has enriched many Peruvian dishes with its sweet and tasty flavor, for example, the famous ceviche. The sweet potato is a tuber native to the tropics of Latin America, central and southern Mexico, and Central America, and it grows at or slightly above ground level. Unlike potatoes, which are tuberous, the part we eat from the sweet potato is its root; this part stores the plant's nutrients, among them a high amount of beta-carotene (an antioxidant with anti-inflammatory properties), especially when it is a darker orange shade. The first roots can be harvested in four months since it grows very fast!

6. PRICKLY PEAR

It is also known as the "sacred tree," and it was used to feed and refresh ancient nomads during hunting season and long travels. It's also the perfect home and host for cochineal, insects used to produce organic dye (used long ago by the Incas!), as well as helping to prevent soil erosion.

It also stands out for its medicinal, anti-inflammatory and analgesic properties as well as its high vitamin, fiber, and mineral content. Be very careful, it has thorns, so if you find it in its natural state, don't pick it with your bare hands (we wouldn't want you to prick yourself!). What you could do is take a leaf from a nearby tree and use it to clean out the thorns and...enjoy!

HELPS PREVENT SOIL EROSION

SQUASH IS AN IMPORTANT SOURCE OF PROVITAMIN A.

ANTIOXIDANTS

7. SQUASH

This huge vegetable grows in the Coast and in the Mountains, and usually weighs between 110 to 130 lbs (50-60 kg), although some varieties in the high Andes (cultivated between 4,920 ft (1500 m) and 9,190 ft (2800 m) above sea level) can weigh more than...220 lb (100 kg)! In Cusco and Puno, as well as in other regions, squash seeds are used for medicinal purposes since they treat parasitic diseases successfully. In fact, squash is an important source of provitamin A, and its intense yellow-orange color indicates a high concentration of carotenoids, antioxidants that help slow aging and prevent heart disease and cancer.

ITS INTENSE YELLOW-ORANGE COLOR INDICATES A HIGH CONCENTRATION OF CAROTENOIDS

8. LUCUMA

LUCUMA'S LOW GLYCEMIC INDEX HELPS STABILIZE THE LEVELS OF SUGAR AND INSULIN IN THE BODY.

Did you know that the *lúcuma* has been used in Peru for many, many years? The oldest evidence of its use are from seeds found in the Guitarrero Cave (dating around 8600 BC and 5600 BC), located in Ancash, Peru.

Archeologists have also found representations of this fruit in ceramics made by the Moche culture, and know that the wood obtained from the *lúcumo* - the tree from which it grows - was used for building the Pachacamac sanctuary.

This fruit, which has a very low glycemic index, helps stabilize the levels of sugar and insulin in the body. It is native to the Peruvian Andes, where it still grows in the wild.

Lima Bean Ceviche

50 min  

INGREDIENTS

- 2 1/3 cups of lima beans
- kernels of 1 cooked Andean corn
- 2 diced tomatoes
- 2 finely chopped cilantro bundles
- 4 tumbos (or 4 limes)
- olive oil
- salt

DIRECTIONS

1. Cook the lima beans in a pot with boiling water for 40 to 45 minutes, until they are tender. Remove from the heat, drain them, and peel them quickly. HELP!
2. Place the lima beans in a bowl and mix them with the Andean corn, tomato, and cilantro.
3. Season with salt, tumbo juice, and olive oil.
4. If you like, you may add diced or finely sliced red onions.

WE SUGGEST SOAKING THE LIMA BEANS THE DAY BEFORE OR FOR AT LEAST THREE HOURS PRIOR TO COOKING THEM.

UTENSILS

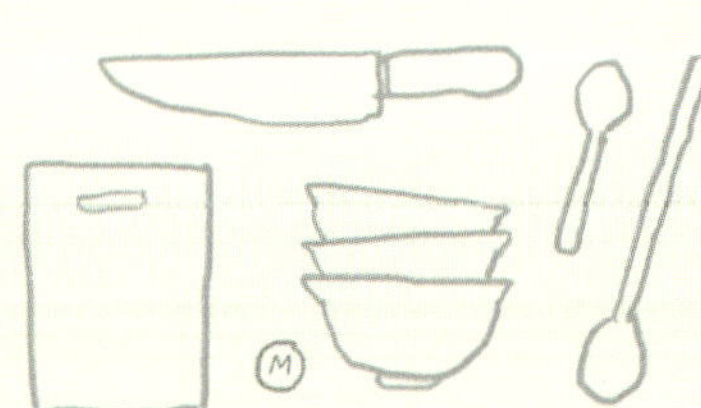

YOU CAN USE BEANS OR CHICKPEAS INSTEAD OF LIMA BEANS
HI THERE.

Causa with Peruvian Yellow Chili Pepper

2 hours |  | 

INGREDIENTS

- 7 medium potatoes
- 2 tbsp. of Peruvian yellow chili pepper paste
- 2 tbsp. of olive oil
- 4 limes
- 2 peeled avocados
- 1 1/2 cups of cooked shredded chicken
- 1 cooked Andean corn cob in kernels
- 1 diced and cooked carrot
- 1/2 cup of cooked peas
- salt

DIRECTIONS

1. Thoroughly wash the potatoes and cook them in a pot with water and salt until the skin opens up. You can poke the potatoes with a small wooden stick to check if they are ready. HELP!

2. Peel the potatoes, place them in a bowl, and use a potato press or mash them with a fork. It is best to do so when they are still hot. HELP!
3. When the mashed potatoes are cold, mix them with the yellow chili pepper paste, olive oil, the juice of three limes, and salt to taste. *Set aside* in a bowl.
4. Blend the avocados with the remaining lime juice and salt to taste. Add a little water to the cream if necessary.
5. To serve, form balls of any size you want with the potato mixture. Flatten them with a spoon and place the chicken on top of that, followed by the avocado cream. Finally, decorate with the Andean corn, diced carrot, and peas.

UTENSILS

TIP
INSTEAD OF CHICKEN, USE CANNED TUNA OR A MIXTURE OF YOUR FAVORITE COOKED VEGETABLES.
LIFE IS LIKE A BOX OF CHOCOLATES.

Tortillas and Fish

INGREDIENTS

- 2 1/4 cups of clean and diced charela filet
- 2 minced garlic cloves
- 2 tbsp. of mustard
- oregano, fresh or dried
- 2 eggs
- 1 tbsp. of plain flour
- 2 1/2 cups of instant oatmeal (oat flour, corn starch, or any other cereal flour)
- olive oil
- 1 avocado
- 2 limes
- 4 corn or flour tortillas
- lettuce, cabbage, or spinach leaves, or any other leaves you prefer, whole or chopped
- salt
- white pepper

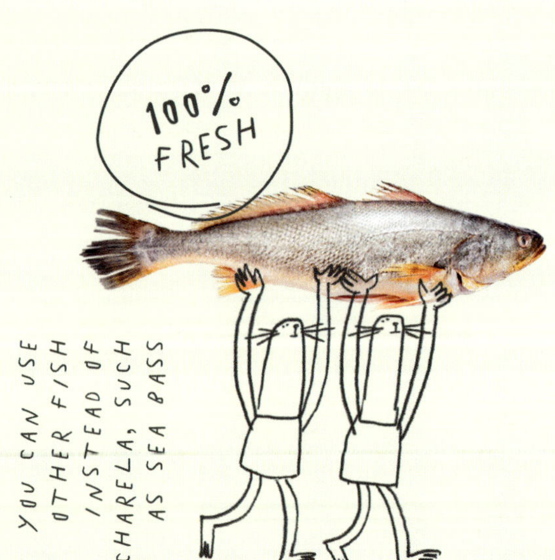

DIRECTIONS

1. Place the diced fish in a bowl and season with salt, pepper, garlic, mustard, and oregano. *Set aside*.
2. In a different bowl, beat the eggs and set aside.
3. Cover a plate with flour and another one with oatmeal.
4. Dip the diced fish in flour and remove the excess. Then, dip it in the beaten eggs and finally pass them through the oatmeal. Carefully press the fish pieces, to maintain the ingredients in place.
5. Heat the oil in a frying pan over medium heat, and fry the fish on both sides. Make it really crunchy! HELP!
6. With a fork, mash the avocado and season with the lime juice and salt. Set aside.
7. Brown the tortillas on both sides in a pan over medium heat without oil, then load them up as you like. You could spread the avocado, then add the fish, and finish it off with the lettuce, or the other way around!

UTENSILS

TIP

THIS RECIPE IS GREAT TO SHARE WITH FRIENDS, HAVE THEM ALL OVER!

Squash and Cheese Stew

INGREDIENTS

- 1 tbsp. of olive oil
- 1/2 diced red onion
- 3 chopped garlic cloves
- 2 tbsp. of Peruvian yellow chili pepper paste
- 2 1/4 cups of diced *macre* squash
- 1 cup of diced *loche* squash
- 1/2 cup of water
- 1/2 of a cob Andean corn in kernels
- 1/4 cup of peas
- 1 diced carrot
- 2/3 cup of diced fresh cheese
- 2 tbsp. of cream cheese
- 1/2 cup of fresh milk
- salt

DIRECTIONS

1. In a medium-sized pot, heat the oil over medium heat. After two minutes, when the oil is very hot, carefully add the onion, garlic, and Peruvian yellow chili pepper paste. Let it cook for 10 minutes. HELP!
2. Add the diced squash and water. Let it cook for 15 minutes, stirring occasionally.
3. Add the corn, peas and diced carrot.
4. When the squash falls apart and the corn is cooked, add both types of cheese, stir with a spoon, and finish by adding the milk. Finally, season with salt to taste.

TIP

IF THE PREPARATION STARTS TO DRY UP, ADD SOME WATER OR BROTH.

UTENSILS

BALANCING COLOR AND FLAVOR!
IN ORDER FOR THE CORN TO BE TENDER, COOK IT FOR 10 TO 15 MINUTES.

Red and Green Prickly Pear Snow Granite

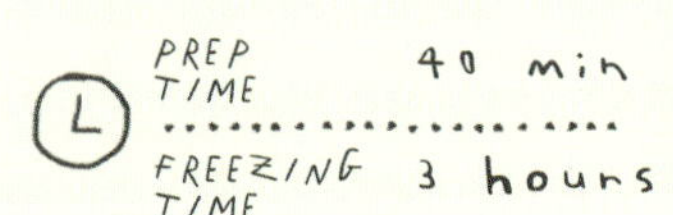

INGREDIENTS

- 1 tbsp. of raw cane sugar
- 1 cup of water
- 10 peeled prickly pears
- 2 limes

TIP

THE PRICKLY PEAR PLANT CAN MEASURE UP TO 16.4 FT (5 M) AND THEIR FRUITS CAN BE RED, GREEN, PURPLE, YELLOW, OR ORANGE.

DIRECTIONS

1. In a medium-sized pot, add the raw cane sugar and water. Place over low heat, and stir with a wooden spoon until the sugar dissolves. Then allow it to *reduce* for 10 minutes, always over low heat, until you get a syrup.

2. Place the prickly pears in the blender and add the freshly made raw cane sugar syrup as well as the lime juice.

3. Blend everything. You may strain the mix or leave it as it is, it will make it crunchier!

4. Pour the mix in a glass container and place it in the freezer for two hours.

5. Remove the container from the freezer and with a fork, scrape the preparation until it resembles snowflakes. Again, place the container in the freezer for about one more hour.

6. Remove from the freezer, scrape again, and ta-da! Enjoy your prickly pear snow.

UTENSILS

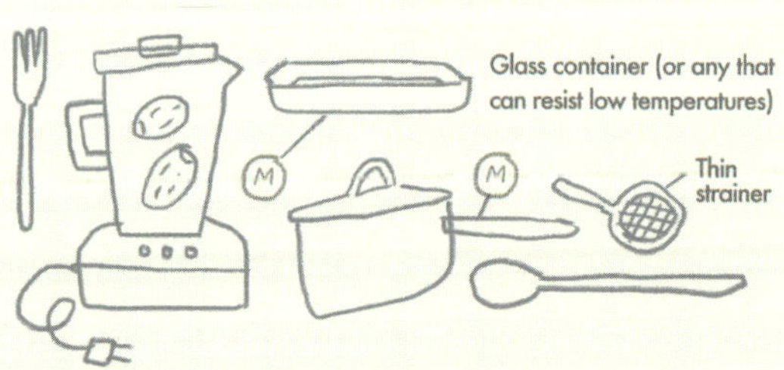

I HAVE CONQUERED ICE!

Sweet Potato Munchkins

PREP TIME .... 1 hour
REST TIME 1 hour

x4

★★★★★!

INGREDIENTS

- 1/4 cup of unsalted butter
- 1 cup of orange and purple cooked sweet potatoes
- 2 2/3 cups of plain wheat flour
- 1 1/2 tsp of dry yeast
- 1 1/2 cup of raw cane sugar
- 1 egg
- 1/10 cup of water
- 8 1/2 cups of vegetable oil
- cinnamon, cacao or powdered sugar
- salt

BANG! HAVE THEM WITH ICE CREAM!

TIP

SWEET POTATOES ARE VERY VERSATILE. YOU CAN USE THEM IN SWEET OR SAVORY DISHES.

UTENSILS

DIRECTIONS

1. Take the butter out of the fridge to allow it to soften. When it is slightly melted, beat it until it is a *buttercream consistency*. *Set aside.*

2. Cut up the sweet potatoes and mash them with a fork until they form a puree.

3. Mix the sweet potato with the flour, yeast, raw cane sugar, and a pinch of salt.

4. Place this mixture in a bowl, add the egg, water, and butter at a buttercream consistency, and beat with an electric mixer until the dough is elastic. You could also place the dough onto a well-floured countertop and knead it with your hands.

5. Shape the dough into small balls, about the size of a medium strawberry, and place them to *rest* in a plate or tray for an hour.

6. Heat the oil in a pan or stewpot, over medium heat for six minutes and fry the balls in batches until they are golden brown. Remove the sweet potato bombs and place them over an absorbent kitchen paper towel to remove any excess oil. HELP!

7. Sprinkle cinnamon, cacao or powdered sugar over the sweet potato bombs.

!!!
I FOUND A SWEET POTATO TREASURE!

Lucuma Gummies

PREP TIME 40 min
REFRIGERATION TIME 10 hours

x4

INGREDIENTS

- 3/4 cup of heavy cream
- 1 medium peeled lucuma (or 1 mango)
- 1 1/2 cups of raw cane sugar
- 4 gelatin sheets or 2 2/3 tbsp. of powdered gelatin

TIP

BE CAREFUL WHEN CUTTING THE LUCUMA. ITS PULP IS VERY DELICATE AND ITS SKIN VERY THIN.

DIRECTIONS

1. In a medium-sized pot, heat the heavy cream over medium heat and add the lucuma pulp and raw cane sugar. Using a hand mixer, bring it all together until the mixture is homogeneous. Remove from the heat and let it cool. HELP!
2. Soak the gelatin sheets in a container with a little cold water, until they soften. Drain and mix them with the previous preparation while it is still warm.
3. Pass the entire mixture through a strainer to avoid any lumps.
4. Pour the preparation in a nonstick mold, ideally made of silicone, and place it in the refrigerator for 10 hours or until the next day.
5. Remove from the mold and cut them up in little squares. You can use molds or cutters of any shape or form you want!

UTENSILS

WEE!
YUMMY, YUMMY, GUMMIES IN MY TUMMY!

MOUNTAINS

The Andes rise between 13,123 FT (4000 m) and 21,981 FT (6700 m) above sea level and its highest peak is the Huascarán mountain, the highest tropical mountain in the world. From these steep mountains and their valleys arise some of the most notable crops that Peru has gifted the world, such as the potato, Andean corn, kiwicha, and quinoa. Join us in discovering these superfoods properties and creating delicacies with them.

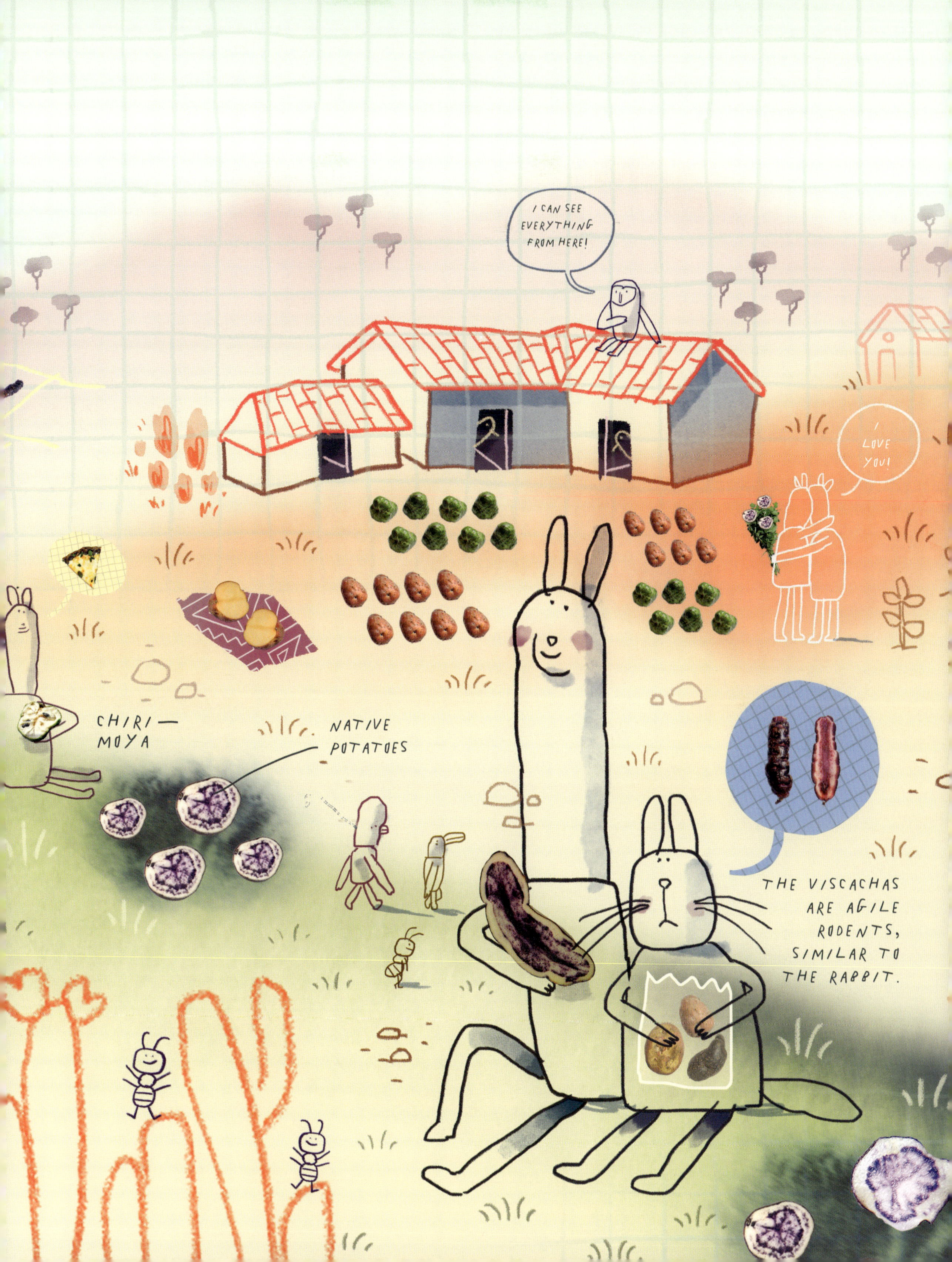
I CAN SEE EVERYTHING FROM HERE!
I LOVE YOU!
CHIRI-MOYA
NATIVE POTATOES
THE VISCACHAS ARE AGILE RODENTS, SIMILAR TO THE RABBIT.

Superfoods from the MOUNTAINS

1. OCA

The potato is the most widely grown tuber in Peru. Do you know which is the second? The oca! Robust and frost-resistant, this tuber is also rich in proteins, has a good balance of amino acids and carbohydrates, and is an excellent source of fiber and antioxidants. It grows in the Andes, in places where the temperature fluctuates between 43 and 59 degrees °F (6-15 degrees °C), and ideally, it should receive sunlight for nine hours a day.

THE OCA IS THE SECOND MOST GROWN TUBER IN PERU!

2. ANDEAN CORN

Do you know how many varieties of corn there are in Peru? About 55! More than in any other place in the world! It is also the crop that occupies the most agricultural land in the country. Its consumption provides high quantities of magnesium, which favors bone growth and muscle formation.

There are many different varieties of corn, but the most prominent is called *piricinco* and it is grown in Huánuco and other Peruvian regions. Its stalk reaches 16,4 ft (5 m) tall, while the smallest corn of all is the *confite puntiagudo*, which is a mere 3.15 in (8cm) long and is grown in Junín, Huancavelica, Ayacucho and Apurímac.

3. NATIVE POTATO

Peru is the leading producer of potatoes in Latin America, and currently 16% of its annual production is native potatoes. Did you know that more than 4000 varieties of native potatoes are grown in the highlands of Peru, Bolivia, and Ecuador? The creation of these many varieties is due to the great knowledge that the local farmers have in managing the fields and the "crossbreeding" of plants to preserve their specific forms, textures, flavors, or colors. It is believed that these wild tubers were grown (or domesticated) for the first time around 8000 years ago by local farmers that lived near lake Titicaca, located between Peru and Bolivia.

They contain high concentrations of zeaxanthin, a carotenoid that acts against visual degeneration, and the purple and red potatoes are found to be a great source of anthocyanins, a natural pigment with antioxidant properties.

PERU IS THE LEADING PRODUCER OF POTATOES IN LATIN AMERICA, AND CURRENTLY 16% OF ITS ANNUAL PRODUCTION IS NATIVE POTATOES.

4. KIWICHA OR AMARANTH

It is considered to be the "food gem" of the Peruvian Andes due to its incredible nutritional properties: it is a powerful cereal as a source of protein and one of the few that is gluten-free. In addition to being a superfood, the kiwicha plant is beautiful, with marvelous flowers in vibrant colors–fuchsias, golden, orange, black, and white–and cylindrical branches that can begin to grow as low as the base of the plant. In some cases, these pretty flowers grow from the main stem and can reach up to 3 ft (90 cm)! It is a powerful pseudocereal.

5. MASHUA

This Andean root is one of the easiest and most efficient to grow as it thrives in rough terrain, growing quickly while successfully competing with weeds. Its cone-shaped tubers are white, yellow, red, or purple, and contain high levels of isothiocyanates (glucosinolates), substances that help keep pests and diseases away from the crops. This is one of the reasons the mashua is traditionally planted interspersed with other crops. The farmers use it to repel insects and pathogens in a natural way.

IN PERU, WE CAN FIND APPROXIMATELY 55 VARIETIES OF CORN. MORE THAN IN ANY OTHER PLACE IN THE WORLD!

6. QUINOA

During the Inca empire quinoa was called "chisaya mama", which means "the mother of all grains," and the Sapa Inca –the supreme leader of the Incas– had the honor of planting the first seed of the season with tools made of gold. Today, this grain is recognized worldwide as a superfood, and comes mainly from the Puno region in Peru. Every 3.5 oz (100 g) of quinoa has between 0.40 oz (12 g) and 0.55 oz (16 g) of protein, and one serving offers 46% of the daily iron requirements (an excellent way to fight anemia!). Also, it is rich in vitamins B2 and B3, magnesium and iron, and has all essential amino acids.

7. CHIRIMOYA OR CUSTARD APPLE

Did you know that the name "chirimoya" comes from the quechua language? *Chiri* means cold in quechua and *muya* means seed. By joining the two words, the name of the most emblematic Peruvian fruit is born, recognized as one of the most delicious in the world. The chirimoya has a high content of vitamin B and calcium, and about 21% of sugars (fructose and sucrose), and is considered a great source of energy.

THE CHIRIMOYA IS CONSIDERED A GREAT SOURCE OF ENERGY.

8. MUÑA

In Peru, it is well known as it helps ease *soroche* (altitude sickness), helps with digestion, and alleviates colds and colics. Its leaves are used to help preserve potatoes and seeds in good condition in the seed beds (shelves in which harvested products are stored in layers to be used as seeds in the next planting season).

Andean Corn Dip

INGREDIENTS

- 1 tsp. of anise seeds
- 1 tbsp. of raw cane sugar
- 6 1/4 cups of Andean corn kernels
- 1 tbsp. of olive oil
- 2 chopped garlic cloves
- 1 diced onion, red or white
- 1/2 cup of heavy cream
- 1/3 cup of butter
- salt

DIRECTIONS

1. In a pot with abundant water, place the anise seeds and raw cane sugar. Add the corn kernels and let it cook over medium heat for eight minutes.

2. Strain and set the corn aside along with one cup of the cooking water.

3. In a frying pan, heat the olive oil and cook the garlic and onion for five minutes. If you wish, you can add a tablespoon of Peruvian yellow chili pepper paste. HELP!

4. Blend the corn, onion, garlic, and chili preparation. Little by little add the heavy cream, and if necessary, pour in some of the cooking water you saved. Blend thoroughly until you get a soft and smooth cream, without any lumps.

5. Strain the mixture and add the butter. Season with salt to taste, and serve with potato or yuca chips, vegetable sticks, or whatever you want!

TIP
FOR THIS RECIPE, PICK CORN COBS WITH THE MOST TENDER KERNELS. THIS WAY, YOU WILL GET A SMOOTHER DIP.
SWOOSHHH

Native Potato Pizza

INGREDIENTS

- 4 peeled native potatoes (pick the most colorful ones: purple, red, yellow, and many more!)
- 2 tbsp. of olive oil
- 1/2 cup of cream cheese
- 1 cup of grated Andean or paria cheese (you can use any cheese that melts evenly)
- oregano, fresh or dried
- salt

TIP

PLACE THE POTATO SLICES ONE ON TOP OF THE OTHER SO THAT WHEN YOU COOK THE PIZZA CRUST, THE CHEESE STAYS IN PLACE.

DIRECTIONS

1. With a *mandoline* slicer or a very sharp knife, slice the potatoes in very thin slices. HELP!

2. Cut a sheet of parchment or baking paper in the diameter of the frying pan you will be using to cook. Arrange the potato slices on top of the paper, forming a circle that will be your pizza crust.

3. Heat the oil in the frying pan over medium heat and add the pizza crust. Cover with a lid and cook for eight minutes on each side. Use a large spatula to help you turn the crust over. It has to be golden and crunchy. HELP!

4. When the pizza crust is ready, add the cream cheese and with the help of a spatula, spread it evenly. Then, add the grated Andean or paria cheese and season with salt and oregano to taste.

5. Cook for two more minutes. Cover the frying pan with a lid, allowing the cheese to melt and serve.

UTENSILS

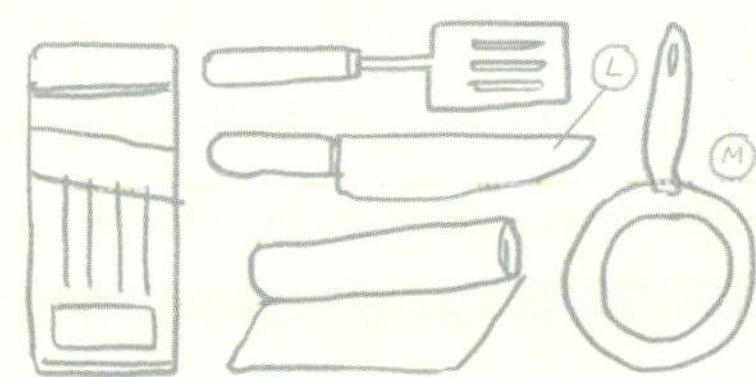

TIP
PICK POTATOES OF THE SAME SIZE FOR YOUR PIZZA CRUST SO IT WILL BE EVEN ALL AROUND.

Oca Doughnuts

1 hour 20 min

INGREDIENTS

- 1/2 cup ocas puree
- 1/3 cup whole milk
- 1 cup whole wheat flour
- 1 tsp. yeast

TIP

WHEN EXPOSED TO SUNLIGHT, THE OCA AS WELL AS THE SWEET POTATO, TURN THEIR STARCH INTO SUGAR, MAKING THEM EVEN SWEETER!

DECORATE YOUR DOUGHNUT ANY WAY YOU WANT.

DIRECTIONS

1. Pour the oca puree in a mixer with the wheat flour and the whole milk (or almomnd milk) until well combined.
2. Place the dry yeast in a separate bowl and pour some warm water to hydrate. Reserve for 20 minutes.
3. Combine the oca mixture with the hydrated yeast and place this mix in a warm environment for 45 minutes.
4. Scoop the dough and place it in doughnut molds or form small balls weighing around 1 tbsp. about the size of a ping-pong ball.
5. Place them on a baking tray covered in parchment paper and take to the oven for 10 minutes at 338°F (170°C). HELP!

UTENSILS

STOP ME
BEFORE I EAT
THEM ALL!

Giant Andean Cereal Cookie

1 hour 20 min | x4 | 

INGREDIENTS

- 1 1/4 cups of Andean grains like quinoa or kiwicha-amaranth, or other cereal flakes (oatmeal, Wheat Bran, etc.)
- 2 cups of quinoa pop
- 1/4 cup of bee honey or agave
- 1 egg
- 2 tbsp. of olive oil
- 1 1/4 tbsp. of peanut or almond butter

IT'S HUGE!

DIRECTIONS

1. In a bowl, mix the Andean grains or cereals with the quinoa, honey, and egg until you get a smooth dough.

2. Stretch out the dough with a rolling pin or your hands on top of a *Silpat* or a nonstick surface, until it is thin.

3. In a large nonstick skillet, heat the oil over medium heat and cook the cookie dough covered with a lid for eight minutes on each side, until it is lightly golden.

4. Once the giant cookie is ready, break it into pieces, spread with peanut butter and enjoy.

5. You can also divide the cookie dough in smaller portions and bake them in a preheated oven at 350 °F (180 °C), for 30 minutes.

UTENSILS

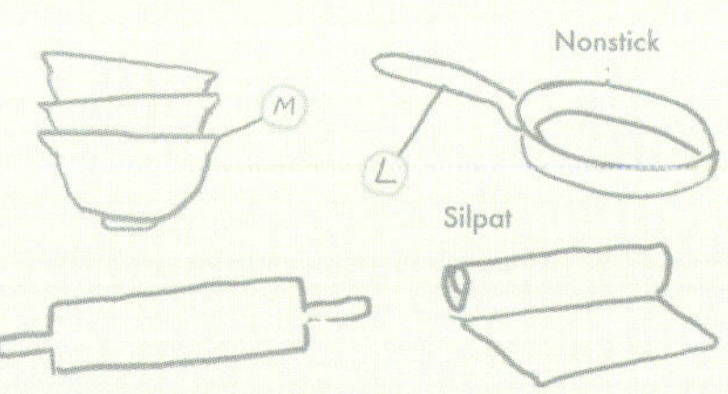

TIP STORE THE COOKIE IN AN AIRTIGHT CONTAINER SO IT STAYS CRUNCHY.

Purple Mashua Ice Cream

PREP TIME 1 hour
FREEZING TIME 10-12 hours
x10
★★★★☆

INGREDIENTS

- 2 1/4 cups of cooked purple mashua (sweet potato or arracacha)
- 2/3 cup of whole milk
- 3/4 cup of heavy cream
- 8 egg yolks
- 1/2 cup of raw cane sugar

SERVE IT WITH AN ICE CREAM SCOOP. IF YOU DON'T HAVE ONE, YOU CAN DO IT WITH TWO SPOONS.

DIRECTIONS

1. Thoroughly blend the mashua. You may add the boiled stock for a creamier texture, but avoid it becoming too watery.
2. Heat the milk and heavy cream in a pot over low heat. HELP!
3. In a bowl, beat the egg yolks with the raw cane sugar until you get a light yellow cream with a dense texture. While beating, add half a cup of the hot milk mixture.
4. Pour the mix in the pot where the rest of the milk mixture is and stir it over low heat until you get a thicker cream.
5. Add the mashua puree and keep stirring over medium heat for approximately 20 minutes, until you get a smooth cream.
6. Pass it through a thin strainer to avoid lumps, pour into a glass ice cream container, and place in the freezer until the next day.

UTENSILS

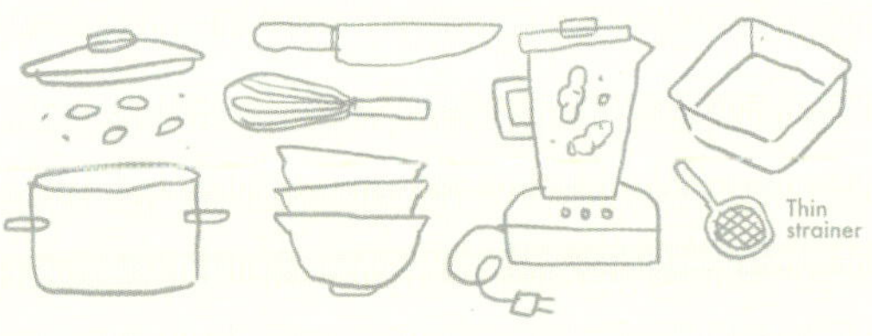

HOME SWEET PURPLE HOME.
TIP
MASHUA IS ALSO DELICIOUS BAKED OR PUREED.

Muña Lemonade

1 hour | x4 | 

INGREDIENTS

- 10 limes
- 3 lemons
- 4 1/4 cups of water
- 1/2 cup of fresh muña leaves
- raw cane sugar or refined sugar
- ice cubes

DIRECTIONS

1. Squeeze the lemons. *Set aside*.
2. Squeeze the limes. Set aside.
3. Pour the water in the blender with the muña leaves, the lemon and lime juices, sugar, and ice cubes.
4. Blend for two minutes, then pass it through a thin strainer.
5. You´re done! You can add more ice cubes when you serve it.

UTENSILS

TIP YOU CAN ALSO PREPARE THIS LEMONADE WITH MINT LEAVES OR LEMONGRASS.

Chilled Chirimoya Cream

50 min

x4

INGREDIENTS

- 1 large chirimoya or custard apple
- 1 tbsp. of lime juice
- 1 2/3 cups of heavy cream
- 2 tbsp. of powdered flavorless gelatin (or two sheets)
- 3 tbsp. of water
- chocolate fudge
- strawberries, blueberries, *aguaymanto* (goldenberry) or your favorite fruit

YOU CAN ALSO SERVE THE CHILLED CHIRIMOYA CREAM IN GLASSES OR CUPS. IN THAT CASE, PUT THEM IN THE REFRIGERATOR FOR AN HOUR.

DIRECTIONS

1. Peel the chirimoya and remove all of its seeds, then blend it with the lime juice.
2. In a bowl, add the heavy cream and mix or whisk until you get a *chantilly consistency*. If you turn the bowl upside down and it stays put, it is ready!
3. In a small bowl, mix the gelatin with the water and place it in the microwave until it dissolves. If you use gelatin sheets, soak them in room temperature water until they are soft.
4. Mix folding the whipped cream with the chirimoya together, and then add the dissolved gelatin. Mix until the preparation is perfectly and completely even.
5. Place the chirimoya cream in a piping bag and do the same with the chocolate fudge. Form fun lines with both on a plate. Let your imagination run wild!
6. On top, place the fruits you chose. Choose your favorite toppings. If you like, you can sprinkle cinnamon on top.

UTENSILS

TIP A CHIRIMOYA WEIGHS APPROXIMATELY 1,10 LB (500 G).

Quinoa Minicakes

50 min | x10 | ★★☆☆☆

INGREDIENTS

- 1 2/3 cups of white or black quinoa flour
- 1/4 cup of raw cane sugar
- 2 2/3 tbsp. of whole milk
- 1 egg
- 2 tsp. of quinoa (kiwicha or cañihua)
- 1/2 tsp. of vanilla extract
- 1/2 tsp. of baking powder

DIRECTIONS

1. Preheat the oven at 350 °F (180 °C).
2. Mix all the ingredients in a bowl with the help of a mixer.
3. Choose your favorite molds, pour the mixture in them, and place in the oven for 25 minutes.
4. You can decorate them with whipped cream, cinnamon, or *powdered sugar.*

TIP

DIFFERENT VARIETIES OF QUINOA EXIST, LIKE BLACK OR RED.

!!!

UTENSILS

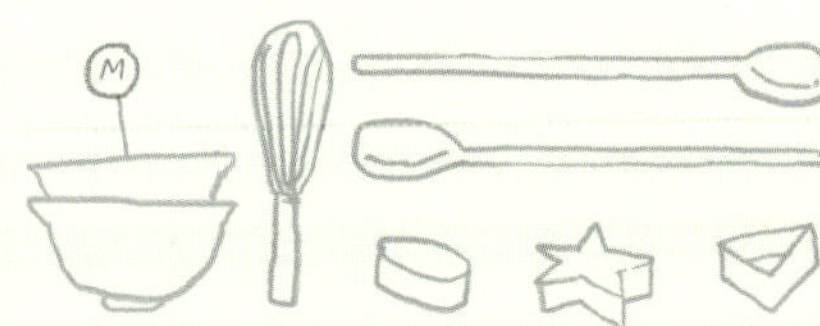

HERE WE GO ROUND THE MULBERRY BUSH, TILL WE GET OUR MINI CAKES!

JUNGLE

Did you know that the Amazon rainforest takes up more than 60% of Peruvian territory? In this immense jungle crossed by the world's largest and most voluminous river, the Amazon river, there are more than 40,000 species of plants, 427 species of mammals, 1300 species of birds and about 2700 different species of fish. Step into the depths Of this jungle with us and taste the wonderful delicacies that can be created with the jungle's delicious ingredients.

THE SARCOPHAGI OF KARAJIA ARE A SET OF COFFINS FROM THE CHACHAPOYAS CULTURE, WHICH MAINLY INHABITED THE AMAZONAS REGION OF PERU.
PE! SHU SHU—
DID YOU KNOW THAT THE AMAZON RIVER IS THE LARGEST AND MOST VOLUMINOUS IN THE WORLD?
THE BEST AVOCADO!
AVO CADO
AVO CADO
I LOVE AVOCADOS!
YUM YUM

Superfoods from

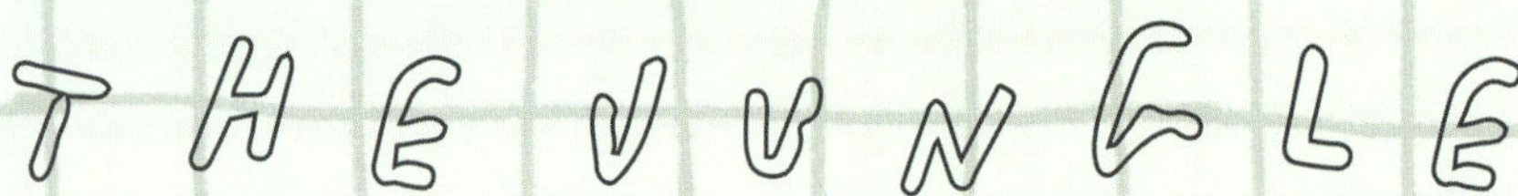

THE YUCA IS BELIEVED TO BE THE OLDEST TUBER IN PERU.

THE CACAO CHUNCHO IS A NATIVE VARIETY THAT HAS A COMPLEX AROMATIC PROFILE.

1. YUCA

This tuber has been grown and eaten in America for many years (did you know that it is believed to be the oldest tuber grown in Peru?), and it is so versatile and strong that it has the ability to grow where no other crops grow (that is one tough yuca!). Eating yuca helps your bones get stronger, improves digestion, and it provides a lot of minerals, as it is rich in calcium and vitamin K.

2. CACAO

Did you know that Peru is one of the main producers of cacao? Did you know that it´s the key ingredient in the world's yummiest sweet: chocolate? The tree of this very important fruit is small and it grows in the tropical jungle of the Amazon basin. There are many groups and families of cacao in Peru and the cacao chuncho has been found to be one of the most "biodiverse". Cacao also contains natural substances that are precursors of serotonin, which help improve your mood. So naturally, eating chocolate makes you happy!

NEW EXPERIMENTS AND WAYS OF MAKING CHOCOLATE SEEK TO USE THE ENTIRE CACAO FRUIT: THE SHELL, MUCILAGE, VEINS (THAT ARE INSIDE THE FRUIT WHERE THE SEEDS ARE ATTACHED), THE SHELL OF THE SEED, AND EVERYTHING ELSE.

THIS FRUIT IS AN EXCELLENT SOURCE OF PROVITAMIN A, VITAMIN B6, VITAMIN C, VITAMIN E, AND IRON.

3. SACHA TOMATE

This fruit (that must not be confused with the tomato!) comes from a small tree or shrub called tamarillo. It is also known as the *serrano tomato*, Andean tomato, or tree tomato. It is usually an intense red color (though you can also find it in purple, orange, or green) and has an intense sweet and sour taste. It is an excellent source of provitamin A, vitamin B6, vitamin C, vitamin E, and iron that help fight illnesses due to its antioxidant properties.

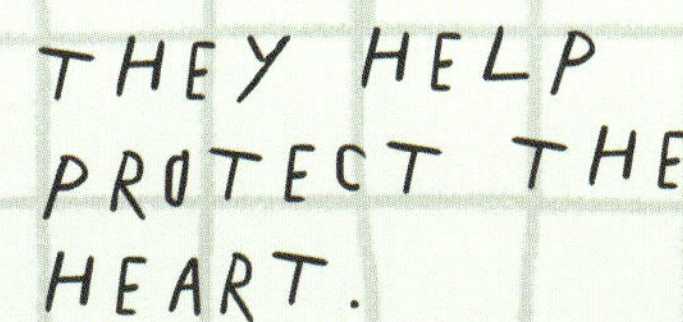

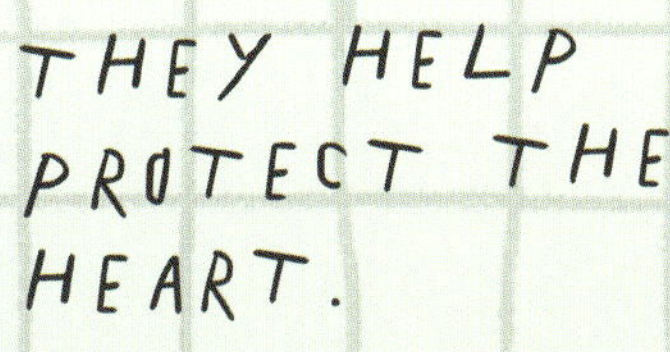

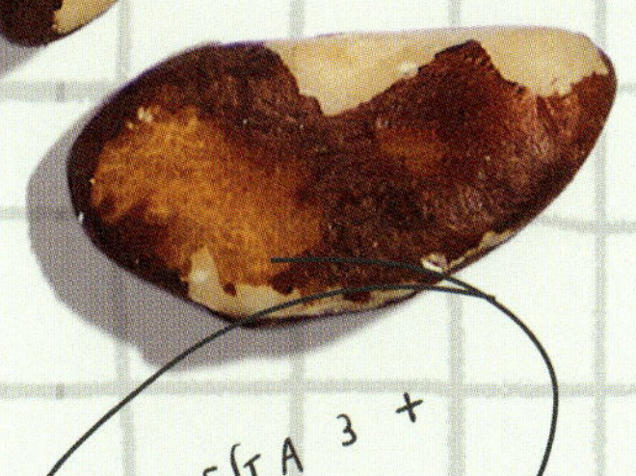

4. AMAZONIAN CHESTNUT OR BRAZIL NUT

The Amazonian chestnut comes from the chestnut tree, which grows in the highest parts of the jungle and can reach up to 165 feet (50 m) in height and live for more than 1000 years. Madre de Dios is the only province in Peru that has enough chestnut trees to harvest this delicious and nutritious nut, which is high in potassium and omega 3 and 6 (these help protect the heart).

5. AVOCADO

Did you know that Peru produces many types of avocados? The most popular are these six: finger or *dedo*, *hass*, *nava*, and *villa campa*, from the coast; and criolla and hass from the jungle. Peru ranks second in the world as a producer and exporter of hass avocados, which grow mainly in the provinces of La Libertad, Lima, Lambayeque, and Ica.

Their high content of healthy fats helps the body's absorption of vitamins K, A, D, and E and some antioxidants like the carotenoids.

Yuca Chips with Avocado Cream and Sacha Culantro

20 min  x4 

INGREDIENTS

- 3 1/5 cups of yuca
- 2 cups of vegetable oil
- 2 limes
- 2 avocados
- 1/4 cup of fresh cheese
- 10 sacha culantro leaves
- 2 tbsp. of olive oil
- salt

DIRECTIONS

1. Peel and slice the yucas in thin slices.
2. Heat the vegetable oil in a pot or pan over medium heat and fry the yuca slices in batches. *Set aside* over parchment paper and season with salt to taste. HELP!
3. Juice the limes and set aside.
4. Peel the avocados and blend them with the cheese, lime juice, and salt.
5. Add the sacha culantro leaves and olive oil to the mixture and keep blending until you get a creamy consistency.
6. With the help of a spatula, pour the avocado cream in a bowl and serve with the yuca chips. You can also have it with potato or sweet potato chips.

UTENSILS

IT SHOULD BE EXTRA CREAMY AND SMOOTH.
TIP
THIS IS AN IDEAL RECIPE FOR SHARING.

Sacha Tomate Red Sauce for Pasta

1 hour  x4 

INGREDIENTS

- 2 tbsp. of olive oil
- 2 chopped garlic cloves
- 1 diced white onion
- 2 1/2 cups of finely diced sacha tomate
- 1 shredded carrot
- 1/2 cup of water or vegetable broth
- oregano, fresh or dried
- raw cane sugar
- salt

DIRECTIONS

1. In a pot, heat the olive oil over medium heat and brown the garlic with the onion for about 10 minutes.

2. Add the diced sacha tomate and shredded carrot. Pour the water or vegetable broth, stir, and let it cook for 20 minutes over medium heat.

3. Season with salt, oregano, and raw cane sugar to taste. Stir and remove from the heat.

4. Serve it with different shapes and sizes of pasta, meatballs, pizza, or whatever you wish!

UTENSILS

TIP
IF THE SAUCE TASTES A LITTLE ACIDIC, MIX SOME PANELA SUGAR WITH IT TO COUNTERACT THE ACIDITY.

Cacao Cream

1 hour |  x4 | 

INGREDIENTS

- 1/2 cup of 72% chocolate
- 1/3 cup of white sugar
- 1 2/3 cups of heavy cream
- 1 1/8 cups of whole milk
- 5 egg yolks

DIRECTIONS

1. In a pot, melt the chocolate over medium heat. Stir with a silicone spatula and *set aside* warm.

2. In a different pot, melt the sugar over low heat, and when it is liquid add the warm heavy cream and mix with a silicone spatula. Then, add the melted chocolate and mix it well.

3. Separately, in a large bowl, mix the milk with the egg yolks. Pour in half of the previous preparation and mix well.

4. Place the contents of the bowl in the pot with the chocolate mixture and beat until you get a thick consistency, or *nappe consistency*.

5. Serve in small containers and place them in a tray with water, cook in a *water bath* in a 212 °F (100 °C) preheated oven for one hour. Wait for the cacao cream to cool before tasting it.

UTENSILS

WHAT A
CREAMY
CENTER!
CRUNCH

Amazonian Chestnut Ice Cream

PREP TIME 1 hour 30 min
FREEZING TIME 10 - 12 hours

INGREDIENTS

- 1/3 cup of peeled Amazonian chestnuts or Brazil Nuts
- 1 cup of whole milk
- 1/4 cup of heavy cream
- 3 egg yolks
- 1/3 cup of raw cane sugar

TIP
TO KEEP YOUR ICE CREAM FROM MELTING, CHILL THE CONTAINERS YOU'LL USE TO SERVE IT.

DIRECTIONS

1. In a bowl, soak the Amazonian chestnuts with the milk for 30 minutes. Then, blend them and pass the preparation through a thin strainer. You now have Amazonian chestnut milk!

2. In a pot, heat the Amazonian chestnut milk and heavy cream over low heat.

3. In a separate bowl, mix the egg yolks with the raw cane sugar and whisk it until the panela is dissolved, obtaining a light yellow cream with a thick texture.

4. Pour part of the warm milk mixture over the beaten yolks and mix well.

5. Pour this mix in the pot containing the rest of the milk mixture and heat it until it gets a thicker consistency (like that of a drinkable yogurt). Use a silicone spatula to keep the mixture from sticking to the pot.

6. Pour the final product in a glass or ice cream container and place it in the freezer until the next day.

UTENSILS

I LOOK THIS PINK.

!!
GRRRR
CRUNCH
YUM
LIMA BEAN
CEVICHE
pg. 20
TORTILLAS
AND FISH
pg. 24
CAUSA WITH
PERUVIAN YELLOW
CHILI PEPPER
pg. 22
NATIVE
POTATO PIZZA
pg. 42
ANDEAN
CORN DIP
pg. 40
CHILLED
CHIRIMOYA CREAM
pg. 52
YUCA CHIPS WITH
AVOCADO CREAM AND
SACHA CULANTRO
pg. 62
QUINOA
MINICAKES
pg. 54

YAY
!!
YUM
YAY
MM
!!
SQUASH AND CHEESE STEW
pg. 26
RED AND GREEN PRICKLY PEAR SNOW
pg. 28
SWEET POTATO MUNCHKINS
pg. 30
LUCUMA GUMMIES
pg. 32
CA
OUGHNUTS
g. 44
GIANT ANDEAN CEREAL COOKIE
pg. 46
PURPLE MASHUA ICE CREAM
pg. 48
MUÑA LEMONADE
pg. 50
ACHA TOMATE
ED SAUCE
g. 64
CACAO CREAM
pg. 66
AMAZONIAN CHESTNUT ICE CREAM
pg. 68

About us

WE WANT YOU TO KNOW A LITTLE BIT MORE ABOUT US, WHAT WE DO, AND WHERE YOU CAN FIND US.

CENTRAL

Peruvian restaurant ran by chefs Virgilio Martínez and Pía León, located in Barranco, the artistic district of Lima. Its culinary proposal is a celebration of the diverse ingredients and ancient traditions Peru has to offer. It has even designed its menu to highlight the different altitudes and ecosystems of the country. It has been recognized as the World´s Best Restaurant by the World´s Best Restaurants Awards 2023.

MATER

This research center was created by Malena and Virgilio Martínez, to investigate the great quantity and diversity of animals, vegetables, ecosystems, and resources from Peru (meaning, its megadiversity). It seeks to learn more about its plants and animals, as well as their different benefits as food sources. It also organizes cultural and artistic projects with various institutions. Mater serves as the headquarters for explorers who love cooking, nature, and nutrition. It is also a source of information for Central, Kjolle, and Mil restaurants. Its headquarters are located in Lima but has another location in Cusco, next to the archeological complex of Moray, inside Mil.

KJOLLE

This restaurant is Pía's creative laboratory, where she and her team exercise their curiosity and skills to create the dishes that earned her the recognition as the World´s Best Chef in 2021, according to the World´s Best Restaurants Organization. She was also awarded the 16th place in The World´s 50 Best Restaurants in 2024.

At Kjolle, you may find flower ice, burnt roots, ashes, extracts, sea lettuce, and fruit nectars from the depths of the Amazon jungle. It's always different. It's always a feast.

CASA TÚPAC

Located in Barranco, Casa Túpac is a venue shared by both Central and Kjolle restaurants and it also serves as the research center for Mater in Lima.
It is no coincidence that before hosting all of this, Casa Túpac was a community cultural center, where artists from different disciplines could create and share their work. This led to a movement that connected them and enriched Barranco's artistic tradition, a tradition that is still carried by the boldest Peruvian chefs, next to apprentices and experts that visit them from around the world.

MIL

A research center and restaurant that investigates and integrates Peru's ancient culinary and agricultural traditions through food and culture. It is located next to the famous ruins of Moray in Cusco, where an Incan agricultural research center once operated centuries ago. At Mil, you may taste some of the most recent culinary creations by Pía, Malena, and Virgilio. Be sure to visit them when you go to Cusco! It entered the World´s 50 Best Restaurants ranking in 2024, in place 73!

ANDEAN OWL
ATHENE CUNICULARIA JUNINENSIS
PUDU
PUDU MEPHISTOPHILES
CARPENTER ANT
CAMPONOTUS SPP
ANDEAN TAPIR
TAPIRUS PINCHAQUE
YELLOW-TAILED WOOLLY MONKEY
LAGOTHRIX FLAVICAUDA
JAGUAR
PANTHERA ONCA
PINK RIVER DOLPHIN
INIA GEOFFRENSIS
SLOTH
CHOLOEPUS DIDACTYLUS
TOUCAN
RAMPHASTOS TOCO
Napeanos
de Pevas
S. Pedro
S. Paulo
Omagua
Yameos
S. Joachim de Omaguas
Amazones
R. Iniate
Rio Yahuari
R. Samiria
Cocamas
Manamabobos
Cunivos
Piros
Cambas
Chunchos
Quimiri

MMM
MMM
2
YUM
YUM
2
1
8
MMM
MMM
1
6
CACAO
CACAO
CACAO